# Love, Relationship and Family Life

## Sparkling Marriage

### How to Reconnect with Your Love

By Lita Caine

# Table of Contents

# Introduction

*"Do what you did in the beginning of a relationship and there won't be an end."*

**— Anthony Robbins**

Why do people think love has a limit? In his book *Human Intimacy*, Frank Cox says, "Falling in love is grand; staying in love is hard work."

This is completely true! Couples love everything complicated, and that's just how relationships are. Love and fights are two sides of the same coin. You cannot have one without the other. There are too many popular sayings about this, such as, *"Where there's hate, there's love"*, *"A couple that fights together, stays together,"* etc.

You know how in school, you used to throw rocks at someone you really liked or teased them mercilessly? Well, this behavior follows you into adulthood but simply adopts a different method.

Have you ever thought about why creating love that lasts is difficult? Even the happiest and best relationships require work because there are plenty of moving parts that never stay the same. A relationship keeps changing because you as a person keep growing.

Here's something that will have the wheels in your brain turning — *love* is described as a <u>verb</u>, which means it is an ongoing effort. You can't call it a one-time moment and be done with it.

Love-at-first-sight is rare but when it does happen, you need to keep the flame burning.

In this eBook, we won't be just giving you anecdotes or tips on how to keep your love alive but will teach you something more important — the language of *love*. Discovered by Gary Chapman, a famous American author and radio talk show host, his book *"5 Love Languages"* tells secrets about how people can strengthen and improve their relationships. Taking a page from his book, we have come up with the perfect guide to help you along your love journey.

## How Relationships Work

No two relationships are the same. Each one has a different dynamic based on the partner's personality and how they treat each other. Couples go through several phases in life that include moments of elation as well as frustration. Most couples don't realize this, but there's a lot of potential to be and stay happy. However, when you get stuck on a problem that can be easily resolved, you tend to fixate on the small things.

Creating intimacy and then maintaining it are two factors that influence love. Intimacy alone is not the driving factor. Sure, every relationship requires a spark. However, if you lack sexual tension, it doesn't mean that you should give up on your partner. Perhaps, something is stopping you and the mental block is keeping you back from going all in.

We do agree that remaining in a toxic and loveless relationship is not healthy. However, you owe it to the years you have spent with your partner. Find out what's causing the strife and hesitation and then get to the root of the matter.

To keep the love boat of your relationship cruising, you need two things — open communication and intimacy. The former involves speaking out loud about your problems and telling your partner what's bothering you and the latter involves opening yourself up and connecting with your partner. It can be either sexual or non-sexual. You need to approach matters in such a way that every conversation with your partner gives you those butterflies you once felt when you met them the first time.

Starting a relationship brings high expectations and excitement. Your emotions are at their peak, and it feels like the intensity of your love will last forever and life is rosy. Along with all this, comes past baggage that is hard to set aside. From your family to your ex-partner and friends, there are numerous attachments that take a back seat to make more room for other important attachments.

For most people, this change takes time and for others, it happens easily. Concern, guilt, jealousy, passion, and fear of loss... these are just some of the emotions that you go through. Then, there's a conflict that occurs at every stage of a relationship.

Those successful at leading a strong relationship know how to keep their calm in a conflict. You will probably get emotional and sometimes even get angry. To understand that your partner's expectations, beliefs, and values are different, and these are the reasons why you are having trouble.

The more you talk about your differences, the better you will be able to deal with any challenges that arise. The main questions that most couples have in mind when starting a relationship are:

- Will they be able to understand me?
- Do I see this relationship going anywhere in the future?
- Do I want to marry?
- Do I want children?
- If I have children, how will I work full-time? Should I work full-time?
- In all these questions, the input of the person you plan to spend your life with is extremely important too.

## A Fulfilling Adult Relationship

Equal rights, equal responsibilities, and equal opportunities — these are the three standing stones of a relationship. Get familiar with them, because most conflicts begin with these and end on them. A fulfilling relationship is one where you respect each other and communicate everything that may cause problems later.

For every couple, the definition of a fulfilling relationship is different. Some of the things that matter include:

- Love (First and foremost)
- Sexual expression and intimacy
- Commitment
- Communication
- Respect and equality
- Companionship
- Compatibility
- Loyalty
- Emotional support

We wouldn't say that a successful relationship has them all because that's not possible. No relationship is perfect. Looking for perfection will leave you nowhere. The image you have in mind of something never comes completely close to reality. The same rule applies to relationships. Have realistic expectations that can be discussed and worked on. For example, expecting that your partner will help you with the house chores is alright. However, expecting that they will do all the chores without your assistance because you work is not reasonable.

Seamlessly melding two minds and hearts together on every level is not realistic! Don't lose sight of the fact, which is you and your partner will butt heads. You need to learn to appreciate and embrace what makes them unique. This is something that you can expect from them too. Don't let the little things drive you apart. There are just some things that cannot be controlled, and accepting that you are not in charge is how you learn to coexist together in harmony.

No one ever said that relationships are easy. They require maximum effort and from both sides to keep the spark alive. Now that you know the basics of how a relationship works, let's start the love journey.

## Fading Sparks

Before you learn to speak the language of love, try to understand what's causing the spark to fade in your relationship. As mentioned earlier, don't see the start of your relationship as the honeymoon phase. As they say, "Make every day Valentine's Day."

People assume that relationships fail because the differences become too big and familiarity makes everything dull. It kills the excitement and leads to predictability. Slowly, you find yourself falling out of love. According to a General Social Survey (GSS), men are more likely to cheat than women.

The reasons — *separation and divorce*

The question is — why do committed people engage in infidelity? If they know that the spark in their relationship is fading, what possesses them to make such a huge decision? Why do their feelings go 0 from 60?

To get to the root of this problem, you need to understand the concept of a *"fantasy bond."*

This concept was coined by psychologist Robert Firestone. His book, *"The Fantasy Bond: Structure of Psychological Defenses"* explains that couples often develop an imagined love life to protect themselves. They substitute it for actual love and whole-heartedly believe that they are in a relationship.

For example, Meredith *loves* love. Her idea of being in love is spending life with a person who will take care of her and make her feel special. However, she has a phobia of commitment. She falls headfirst into a relationship without fully knowing Mark.

Even though there's no connection, she convinces herself that Mark's the one because he fulfills her needs.

A fantasy bond usually exists when reality is replaced by practicality. You go through the motions of a relationship, but there are no emotions involved. Childhood experiences, repeating patterns that are hard to break out of, and fear of ending up alone are usually the factors that drive a fantasy bond.

Coming to the point — if you are at a stage in your relationship where comfort is all you seek and spontaneity has vanished, you need to reevaluate your bond now! The longer your relationship continues in this manner, the more difficult it will become for you to stay committed. The distinction between you and your partner will start with small fights, proceed to the blame game, and lead to full-blown-out screaming matches. One of you will follow the line of predictability to avoid causing any ripples in the relationship. However, what you don't see here is that you are slowly losing your identity.

To work on your fantasy bond, if there's one, you need to first find out what's causing you to fall out of love.

## Signs That You Are Falling Out of Love

The early stages of a relationship are full of magic. The appreciation and affection are endless. However, the reality is that every person changes over time and so does the bond between them. This doesn't necessarily have to be bad. All you need to do is stay on the roller coaster because the fun is in the twists and turns that come after a steady ride.

Many signs of a failing relationship are fixable. The only thing you need to do is openly discuss what's bothering you. Show your partner you're willing to change and ask the same from them. At some point, your emotions might overwhelm you, so share the burden.

Let's look at the most common signs of a failing relationship:

### 1.  When "We" Turns Into "I"

Togetherness and unity are two words you need to familiarize yourself with. If you think of your partner and yourself as a single unit, your love is there. It's just hidden beneath a few layers, waiting to be discovered. However, if most of your sentences start in "I," that means their goals and yours are not the same.

The best way to turn "I" into "we" is to keep your partner in mind in your decisions. Ask yourself, *"If I do this, will they mind?"*

*"Perhaps, making a decision together will be better."*

*"I better ask them for their opinion."*

Involve your partner in everything you do to show them you are 100% committed.

### 2.  You Feel Lonely

Partners who are irrevocably in love share one common trait — they want to tell each other everything, starting from what they did the entire day to what they ate and anything exciting that happened. When you're more interested in taking a nap after getting home from work, then deep down, you are trying to avoid your partner. Even though you are sitting right beside your partner, you feel as if you are all alone. Find out the cause behind it, and you will know why you are acting so indifferent.

### 3. *Your Weapon of Choice in a Fight – Silence Over Disagreement*

In a healthy relationship, couples argue. Yes, no one wants to argue because it always leads to a difference in opinion, but this also strengthens your bond. Let's assume that you and your partner got into a fight. Instead of talking it out or apologizing, you take a vow of silence. This gives your partner the wrong impression, and instead of clearing the air, they talk to other people.

The fact that you are silent shows you don't care. It means you're becoming complacent. The longer the silence continues, the bigger the problem gets. When a pattern develops, you find solace in the knowledge that if you don't talk, things won't escalate.

### 4. *The Little Things Don't Matter Anymore*

You know those little tokens of affection that let your partner know that you care about them… if these disappear, you are in big trouble. A kiss on the lips goodbye, paying compliments to bring a smile on their face, and rubbing their forehead the moment you see them in pain — these are the little things that strengthen a relationship.

If you are least bothered to ask your partner about a big day or something important in their life, you need to think fast about where this relationship is going. This act of tuning out shows that you are disinterested and couldn't care less.

## 5.  *There's Zilch Sexual Attraction*

As much as comfort and open communication are important to keep the relationship care running, so is sexual attraction. Do you tingle when your partner is nearby? Do you blush when your partner gives you a heated look?

It's alright if your sex life has hit a temporary pause due to some problems. However, when the act becomes a chore, it means the excitement is gone.

The biggest sign that you are falling out of love with your partner is you no longer look at them with love in your eyes. Meaning — you are friend-zoning them. In a relationship, there's one thing that every partner deserves: *respect*. As we said, every couple fights but losing sight of the argument and calling each other names is what takes it too far. You need to make sure that you are not bringing your past hurts to the present because that will only complicate matters.

## The Stepping Stones of a Strong Relationship

If you believe that disillusionment and problems are inevitable, you are right. However, the problems themselves are not the cause of distress in your relationship. Again, know that all couples fight. Your satisfaction is dependent on a few different things, such as:

- How much power do you give to your problems?
- How do you deal with your feelings?
- How do you communicate and act under stress?
- Where do you focus all your attention to stop yourself from lashing out?

Keep in mind that every relationship has its ups and downs. You will come to a point in your life where you will ask yourself: *Is this relationship worth all the trouble? Am I happy?*

If your heart isn't in it, the answer will probably be "no."

But why? Have you ever thought of that?

Let's take a look at a situation:

*Sara and Connor are madly in love with each other. Connor adores Sarah and fulfills her every need. He knows he can depend on her in a tough situation. She's the type of person who doesn't demand much, and that makes Connor feel complete.*

So, why isn't Sarah happy in the relationship?

That's because both of them failed to climb the stepping stones of a relationship! These metaphorical stones represent the important parts of a relationship that allow you to tackle problems one at a time. The concept behind these stepping stones is that to be healthy and whole as a couple, you need to first pay attention to yourself, then to your partner, and finally to your relationship.

Let's look at these stepping stones:

### Individual Growth – Feeling Complete as a "Person"

Do you depend on your partner for every little thing? Has this led to certain unmet expectations? If you are simply trying to fill a void in your life, your demands are putting too much pressure on your partner. Instead of going down this path, start practicing self-love. In a relationship, partners need to stand equal rather than against each other. Do things that will allow you to grow individually. This will allow you to bring back confidence in your life.

### Collective Growth – Feeling Complete as a "Couple"

Common goals are the biggest sign of collective growth. If you and your partner desire the same thing, you both will stand hand in hand and proceed together. This doesn't mean that you aren't allowed to have individual desires. Only that when you share an interest, things get much easier and your bond gets stronger. In the former case, support your partner by showing them that you believe in their dream and would like them to succeed.

### Find Your Spot

What's the one place in your house where you feel comfortable with your partner? Is it the bedroom or the living room? The "spot" that we are referring to is a haven where you feel one with your partner. It's where you don't fight and never argue. It's where the good times are spent. In this spot, you are one with the other… we know it sounds a bit Mr. Miyagi but you truly do sit peacefully and stay content in each other's presence. This stepping stone cannot be climbed until and unless you have learned to stand on equal footing.

## Connection – Complain Constructively

When you have a strong connection with your partner, you do not argue over the little things. You have probably heard this phrase, "Love and hate go hand in hand."

Like fights, complaints are normal in a relationship. However, the key to complaining in a calm and collected manner is to address the problem at hand rather than raising your voice in anger and name-calling. Never fight when you are angry because then, you aren't arguing about the matter at hand but past problems, which you throw at your partner to make a point.

## Communication

The final stepping stone is communication, which is the most important. There's a reason why it's the last because to communicate with your partner freely and openly, you need to first feel secure in the relationship.

Let's assume that something your partner said has been bothering you for a while. Instead of talking it out with your partner, you pout all day and wait for the chance to attack your partner when they ask if something is troubling you. The silent treatment and glares continue for a quite a while with no explanation. Confusion builds up like gas in a shaken Coca-Cola bottle and when you finally open your mouth, words spill out that are meant to hurt. When communicating, always lay down the ground rules:

- No judgment
- No criticism
- No blaming

Once you climb these stepping stones, you will be ready for the next chapter in your life. Keep in mind — if you aren't open and honest with your partner, you will never be content with what you have. You will always yearn for more and create "what-if" scenarios in your mind.

Every relationship grows steadily. Yes, love at first sight is real but for some people, it doesn't happen instantly. Though they are with their partner for months or years, there comes a moment where they get hit with the realization that if it weren't for their partner, they would still be sitting at home and watching reruns of their favorite TV shows. Usually, relationships fail because there's no commitment. Your ability to stick with your partner through thick and thin is what matters in the end. Communication and compromise go together. You won't be able to make your relationship last longer if you can't talk about your problems or compromise on the little things.

## Speaking the Language of Love

Love is not eternal! People easily fall out of love. Watching movies and TV shows, we have developed this image of love that it's the most magical thing that changes your life, makes you daydream all time, etc. Remember Giselle from *Enchanted*? After being thrown into a strange world, her one-and-only goal was to find Edward. When Robert asks her how long she has known Edward, Giselle replies, "One whole day." It's then that Robert tells Giselle to not rush into things, and if indeed Edward is her one true love, he wouldn't mind taking her on a date and talking.

This, right here, captured what love is all about — *communication*. It is the most powerful tool in a relationship!

Think of it as the magic recipe, which can make your relationship last longer. Do you know why couples don't communicate with each other openly? It's because not only are they afraid to say the truth out loud but they also feel uncomfortable putting themselves in a vulnerable position. Theorists and professionals have come up with hundreds of concepts that are based on love and all of them target one thing — whether a couple will make the journey to the "I Dos" or not.

Are you ready to find out how you have been communicating all wrong with your partner for the past years? Let's begin

Answer this question first — you love your partner, right?

Then why aren't you both on the same page? People experience love differently. There's the couple that says it all through their eyes, the one that finishes each other's sentences (so annoying), the one where a partner does all the talking and the other listens, and the list goes on. These couples all have a way to communicate what they are feeling but the message gets lost in the translation.

This is where Dr. Gary Chapman, the author of the book titled *"The 5 Love Languages®."* Released in 1995, this book quickly became popular as it addressed the core problems every couple faces. In his book, he explained that the key to making your relationship last long is a love language that focuses on making your partner feel loved and appreciated.

Often, showing affection becomes a guessing game. You start to doubt yourself whether your partner will appreciate your efforts or brush them aside with a simple "Thank You." Dr. Chapman believes that if a person can understand how their partner likes to be loved then there won't be unmet expectations. This will allow the couple to live in harmony and resolve any problem even before it becomes one.

The 5 Love Languages® helps identify the cause of conflicts, teach, give, receive and accept love in meaningful ways and discover your long-lost connection with your partner.

## The Love Language Quiz

Before we begin, let's take a short quiz to find out what's your love language and how you should use it to build a connection with your partner.

1. Gender

☐ Male

☐ Female

2. Age

☐ 18 – 24

☐ 25 – 34

☐ 35 – 44

☐ 45+

**3.** Are you married or in a relationship?

☐ Married

☐ In a relationship

**4.** Which one of the following gestures feels more meaningful to you?

☐ When my partner texts me, emails me, or sends me flowers for no reason

☐ When I and my partner hug

**5.** Which one of the following gestures feels more meaningful to you?

☐ Spending some alone time with my partner

☐ My partner helping me out with some of my work

**6.** Which one of the following gestures feels more meaningful to you?

☐ When my partner gives me a gift because he/she loves me a lot

☐ When I spend my leisure time doing fun activities with my partner

7.  Which one of the following gestures feels more meaningful to you?

☐ When I and partner touch each other

☐ When my partner helps me with the household chores like cooking, cleaning, dusting, laundry, etc.

8.  Which one of the following gestures feels more meaningful to you?

☐ My partner puts his/her arm around me

☐ My partner surprises me with a gift

9.  Which one of the following gestures feels more meaningful to you?

☐When my partner and I are holding hands

☐ When we both are sitting together in comfortable silence and doing nothing

10. Which one of the following gestures feels more meaningful to you?

☐ When my partner says, "I love you."

☐ When my partner gives me a gift

There's no right or wrong answer in this quiz. The purpose of it is to find out how you communicate with your partner so that you can work more on that particular love language.

## The 5 Love Languages®

To understand the results of your quiz, you need to first know about the five love languages.

### 1. *Words of Affirmation*

Anything from a complimentary phrase to a verbal appreciation that makes your partner feel special comes under *words of affirmation*. For example:

*You look stunning*

*That dress looks amazing on you*

*Seeing your face brightens my entire day*

This is the language that affirms to your partner that they are the sun and moon in your life.

### 2. *Acts of Service*

You know how they say, "Actions speak louder than words?"

Well, if you can't put your feelings into a sentence or even write them down, the best way to show them is through a gesture. *Acts of service* tell your partner how much you love them and would do absolutely anything to make them happy. For example:

*You come home tired from work and see the dinner table ready with your favorite meal.*

*Your partner worked all night to repair the bathroom shelves. Exhausted now, they are lying on the couch and trying to sleep. You go over to them and massage their feet and hands.*

### 3. *Quality Time*

Sitting down with your partner and opening up to them about your troubles without any fear is what *quality time* is all about. The more you talk freely with your partner, the more they will share themselves with you. Isn't that what all couples want? — a strong connection with their partner. Here's how you can spend quality time with your partner:

*Taking on a DIY project that you both love.*

*Watching Netflix while cuddling on the couch.*

*Surprising your partner on date night by taking them somewhere they have always wanted to spend more time with them.*

### 4.  *Physical Touch*

Someone who loves actions more than words speaks through physical touch. Aside from sex, there are plenty of ways to initiate this love language. Here's how you can show your partner that you love them:

*Holding hands while watching a movie.*

*Casually running your hand through your partner's hair.*

*Touching them every moment you get a kiss on the cheek when passing in the hallway.*

For a person who loves physical touch, their ideal date night would be to spend the evening cuddling on the sofa.

### 5.  *Receiving Gifts*

No matter how small or big your gift is, as long as it has a deep meaning attached to it, your partner will love it! Gift-giving is a symbol of affection and love. The person receiving the gift not only treasures the item but also remembers the time you gave it and the efforts made. So, don't wait for special occasions such as Valentine's Day or your anniversary to buy your partner something. There are plenty of ways you can show your love such as:

*Bringing a box of their favorite sweets home while coming from work.*

*Giving them a bouquet of flowers for no reason.*

*Giving them something special they have been hinting at for a long time.*

And that's how you communicate with your partner! As mentioned earlier, communication is the key to keep a relationship strong and going forever. Often couples overlook it because they don't want to make themselves look vulnerable and that's their biggest mistake.

The good news is that therapists and professionals have come up with unique communication exercises that couples can easily try at home to resolve problems. Let's take a look at them:

## 6 Communication Exercises to Build Your Connection

Communication exercises should be engaging and fun. We don't want you to just sit on the couch and simply start talking. At one point, the talk will turn into an argument and you will abandon your seat. To keep the conversation flowing you need to be physically and emotionally present. Only then you will be able to open your heart, listen to your partner without any judgment and respond in a manner that will resolve things rather than escalate them.

To help you tackle different issues, we have come up with three different categories of communication, which include appreciation, one-on-one conversation, and intimacy. The following exercises will help you understand how to tackle a problem through communication:

**Exercises to Improve Intimacy**
*Exercise #1*

*Soul Gazing and Extended Cuddle Time*

Did you play the "Don't Blink" game as a child? If yes then this will be pretty easy for you. If you haven't built up the confidence to have an honest conversation yet then you can communicate without saying a word. This is how soul gazing and cuddling works.

The deep connection that is built with soul gazing might make you feel vulnerable but push through the uncomfortable feeling and lay yourself open in front of your partner. Here's how to start:

- Sit somewhere comfortable so that your knees are touching, preferably your bedroom or the living room couch
- Inhale deeply and then look into your partner's eyes. This is no contest so you are allowed to blink
- Refrain from talking
- When the silence becomes uncomfortable, just blink but don't break eye contact

Continue this exercise for at least 5 minutes and all the while, think of all the good memories you have spent with them and how much you love them.

When you break eye contact, take a deep breath and cuddle each other. Do not pick up your phone or tablet or do anything else. Stay where you are and be content in each other's embrace. Listen to your partner's heartbeat and when you feel yourself calming down, go to sleep. A great way to make your cuddle time more intimate is to pick a song you both love and play it in the background.

*Exercise #2*

*Play Multiple-Choice*

Sounds boring, right? In the movies, when a woman is sitting on her man's lap, words come easily because of the intimacy brought by the closeness. So, we decided to come up with a fun way to ease the tension and make the thought of intimacy more exciting.

This exercise is based on the five love languages. Here's how to play it:

Pick your partner's love language and ask them the following questions:

Words of Affirmation: What makes you feel happier and appreciated? When I:

A. Compliment you
B. Tell you that you have been doing a great job personally and professionally
C. Tell you cheesy love jokes

Quality Time: What do you want to do today?

- A.   Go for a romantic dinner
- B.   Go for a long drive
- C.   Do an activity of your liking together

Physical Touch: How would you like to spend this evening?

- A.   An intimate massage
- B.   A bath together with chocolate-covered strawberries and champagne
- C.   Play strip poker

Acts of Service: How would you like me to help you today?

- A.   Make dinner and wash the dishes
- B.   Work on your office project with you
- C.   Help you clean the house

Receiving Gifts: Is there something that you want?

- A.   How about I buy you that ring you liked in the mall a few days back
- B.   Would a new dress and a pair of heels make you happy?
- C.   Here's a bouquet of flowers and a box of chocolate for you

You can come up with different questions according to what your partner loves and then give them multiple choices to pick what they like the most.

**One-On-One Conversation**

*Exercise #3*

*The Miracle Question*

The miracle question also called the "what-if" question is a way to think about your future. It allows you to explore uncharted boundaries in your life so that you can learn about your partner's dreams and desires. One of the biggest plus points of this exercise is that you both get to discover new things about each other.

This exercise is pretty simple, though it can be a little difficult to answer the question. The following is how the miracle question is phrased:

*"Suppose a miracle happens in the night. You are overjoyed and can't wait to start the new day. How will your life be different the next day? Would it be good or great?"*

The answer needs to come from the heart and sometimes can be a little daunting because you are laying yourself open. However, the result is that you and your partner become a lot closer because you learn new things about each other's hopes and dreams.

*Exercise #4*

*The CEO Meeting*

Many couples lead jam-packed lives with work, events, activities, and obligations. If you are lost in this chaos, a CEO meeting will help you connect without any stress.

So, what do we mean by a CEO meeting? It's an exercise that you do with your partner where no kids are present and without any distractions such as laptops, tablets, and phones. Schedule a small chunk of time, like 30 minutes, and make sure that nothing in your routine derails this meeting. The meeting should be held at least once a week so that you can tell each other a good amount of things that happened in your life. This doesn't mean that you don't share anything in between.

Questions to ask in this exercise include:

- Is there anything you would like to say before we start this meeting?
- Where are we emotionally today?
- Was there anything I did in the past that made you feel incomplete? Do you want to talk about it?
- Do you find my efforts lacking?
- Is there any way I can make you feel loved, more so than I usually do?

The layout is not set in stone. You can come up with questions that address your daily life or anything important you've been meaning to talk about with your partner.

The answer to these questions will help you have a productive and healthy discussion about your relationship and yourself with your partner.

## Appreciation Exercises

*Exercise #5*

*Accepting Your Mistakes*

In a relationship, it often happens that couples blame each other even when they know they are at fault. This not only builds up tension but also resentment, because your partner feels they are always wrong, when in fact they are not. Like you feel the need to be appreciated, so do they.

First, you should start with a clean slate. Past mistakes should stay where they are: in the past! Then, take the following step:

**Acknowledge your mistake:** It's time to start taking responsibility for the hurt you cause. You can do this by saying:

- *I am sorry. I shouldn't have done…*
- *I messed up…*

**Explain why you made the mistake:** Let your partner know that it wasn't your intention to hurt them. You can do this by saying:

- *By the time I realized my mistake, it was too late…*
- *I was afraid that you would…*

**Express remorse:** Tell your partner how you felt after making the mistake. You can do this by saying:

- *I am embarrassed at the way I acted.*
- *I feel ashamed that I even did such a thing.*

**Make amends:** Is there any way the problem can be fixed? Ask your partner for directions.

**Remember:** When admitting to your mistakes and apologizing, always start your statements with "I". The apology needs to come from the heart and should feel personal. Moreover, it should also show the partner that you feel remorse and take full responsibility for your actions.

*Exercise #6*

*Keep a Journal*

Journaling is a great way to strengthen your relationship. Problems occur when couples are too afraid or shy to say things out loud. Hence, writing your thoughts on paper and then allowing your partner to read them is such a great idea. It helps you lift this weight off your chest, allowing you to deal with the situation without any confrontation. Moreover, if you are the type of person who often jumps to conclusions just by reading one's expressions, this exercise will prove to be very successful for you.

Through communication exercises, you get to learn a lot about your partner. Every time something new is revealed about them, you will understand your partner's actions better. With an open and honest conversation, you will be able to tackle a problem calmly so that there's no fallout. However, keep in mind that trust is a fragile thing. Never make a mistake you can't come back from because it can change the dynamics of your relationship.

# How to Make Your Love Grow – The Do's and Don'ts of a Relationship

The first glance of your partner as your eyes met their's, that shy smile, the first move... such intimate moments are remembered fondly. No matter who takes the first step, the fear and excitement felt in that moment is what you cherish every day in your life. However, when these moments are colored by mistakes, it becomes difficult for you to remember the good in your relationship.

How about not making mistakes in the first place? Easier said than done, and near-impossible! But that's not what we want you to strive for, because that's a battle already lost. What you can do is take a few precautions to make sure your romance is kept alive. You will find plenty of advice online telling how to patch up your relationship, but most of it is impractical. Every couple goes through difficult times, and the real challenge is to not go into your overwhelmed and confused feelings.

So, here are a few dos and don'ts of a relationship:

## Do's

**Do** *Try to Arrive on Time:* **One of the biggest mistakes that many partners make is that they keep the other partner waiting. Don't think that making excuses will save you. However, informing your partner beforehand that you might be late is acceptable. We would still advise that you don't make plans that you can't stick to.**

**Do** *Learn How to Compromise:* **One of the biggest causes of silly fights is not being able to understand each other. When you and your partner are not on the same level, neither of you**

agrees to give in. For example, you have been planning a weekend vacation for quite some time. Suddenly, your partner tells you that they want to use the saved money for something else. You don't agree. A fight ensues and your partner says that they won't be going on the trip. This situation could have been easily avoided if one of you had agreed with the other. Compromises are hard but if you show your partner that you are ready to sacrifice your happiness for theirs, they will reciprocate in the same manner.

**Do** *Treat Each Other the Same Way When You First Met:* Every day marks the new beginning of your love life. There are endless possibilities to make your partner feel special. These gestures should not be reserved just for the wooing days. As your love develops, so do your expectations, and this is both right and wrong. It's right that your partner wants you to reciprocate their feelings but wrong that sometimes, they have unrealistic expectations about this reciprocation, which can result in unmet needs. To avoid this mess, stay the way you were when you first met your partner and shower them with the same intensity of love or more.

**Do** *Pay Attention to Their Emotional Needs:* Your sex life is amazing. You can't keep your hands off of each other. The moment you enter the bedroom, BOOM, sparks start flying. However, when it comes to really knowing what your partner wants from the heart, you are clueless. Their physical needs are of as much importance as their emotional ones. So, don't neglect them! Every now and then check in with your partner to let them know that you are there for them. Even the smallest gesture will make them feel better.

**Do** *Help Push Each Other Towards Their Goals:* A relationship faces new challenges every day. There will always be some hurdle that will stop you from reaching your goal. The same goes for your partner. So, help each other out by giving a vote of confidence and making sure that you both know that you believed in each other.

**Do** *Make Yourself Vulnerable In Front of Your Partner:* Often couples shy away from showing vulnerability, not because they feel uneasy about it but because they think it's a weakness. If a partner does not feel secure in their relationship, they won't talk about their hopes and dreams, fearing that the other partner might reject them. Try once voicing your fears and the rest will come easily to you. Your partner will take a sigh of relief because then they will be able to truly help you in every manner.

## Don'ts

**Don't** *Let Your Feelings and Emotions Buildup:* Negative emotions are like a ticking time bomb. They fester inside you and always come out at the wrong moment. This is not something you want to bottle because when these feelings make an appearance, they have the power to break your relationship. If something your partner did bothered you, speak up immediately. Bringing up things from the past can feel like you are trying to settle a score.

**Don't** *Let Yourself Loose:* It's only been a year into your relationship and you have gained 15 pounds. You don't take care of hygiene and looking good for your partner is seldom on your mind. Some people see this as a level of comfort that is "relationship goals." So not true! Just because you have found your soul mate, it doesn't mean that you should neglect yourself. Your relationship has just begun so it's time to put in extra effort in every way to show your partner that you are fully committed.

**Don't** *Exploit Your Partner's Weakness:* What's the one thing your partner can't handle? When they see you cry or when they feel they have let you down? Perhaps, their one and only mission is to make you happy. No matter what the case, using any of these points as leverage makes you a bad partner. If they show you their weakness, it means they trust you. Don't exploit that trust because it's fragile. Always try to motivate them rather than bringing them down.

**Don't** *Let Jealousy Be the Driving Factor in Your Relationship:* You heard a silly rumor about someone coming on to your partner and now you are blowing up their phone to ask them the deets. Not done! The question you should be asking yourself right now is, "Do I trust my partner?" If the answer is "yes" then you don't need to worry about anything. However, if your heart says "no" then the moment your partner will enter the house, you will pick a fight with them. Instead of going off the hook, why not express your feelings? Seems so simple, right? Well, it is... try it.

**Don't** *Pull Them in Your Unhappiness:* As mentioned earlier, every couple faces a lot of problems. Their ability to come out unscathed is what pushes them one step closer to having a relationship that is full of happiness and satisfaction. If you fail at something, don't blame your partner. If you are doing this then you are not in the right mind space to continue your life with them. You might need a break and some alone time to yourself may do you a world of good.

***Don't*** *Start Discussing the Future on Your 1st, 2nd, or 10th Date:* You just met and you are already talking about where you will buy a house and where you will vacation? Look fast — your partner just ran off like Wile E. Coyote in that Looney Tunes Road Runner cartoon. This is bound to happen because most people are afraid of commitment. If you come on too fast and strong, you will lose your partner. So, give them some space and let the relationship take its natural course.

No two relationships are the same. You have to find out what works for you best and then proceed with it to make your relationship strong. Nobody knows the dynamics of your relationship better than you. So, instead of listening to neighborly advice, try implementing these dos and don'ts to see how they turn your relationship around.

## Why Strive for a "Good-Enough" Relationship

You are probably wondering what's a "good-enough" relationship, right? What is the first thing that comes into your mind when you hear these two words?

- *Compromise*
- *Letting go of your dreams*
- *Disappointment that you asked for more and got less*

True love is quite exhilarating. However, according to relationship therapist John Gottman, a good-enough relationship is a benchmark that couples should strive for.

### Understanding a Good-Enough Relationship

Let's talk about what exactly this relationship entails. Though the term is contradictory, it actually has a positive meaning.

Gottman explains that a good-enough relationship is not about settling for less but appreciating what you already have. Often people don't value what they hold dear. The moment it's taken away from them, only then do they realize its importance. The same falls for partners in a relationship. Your relationship will last longer and become stronger with time if you just realize what's in front of you.

For example, your partner treats you with respect and affection. These are the two essential ingredients that complete a relationship. However, whenever your partner does something for you, you feel like they could have done better. This means that you have unrealistic expectations that usually come from movies and TV shows. Your life cannot be like a Disney movie, as much as you would like it to be.

We are not saying that you need to stop having expectations but simply lower them to a level that your partner can easily fulfill.

Do you ever say to your partner — "I love you but… "

Why does your declaration of love have a hiccup? Yes, every relationship has a bad side but why don't you look at the good side for a change? Things will seem much better and brighter!

The following example will help you understand what we are trying to say:

*George and Elizabeth have been in a relationship for a year. They have had their ups and downs. After a hectic weekday, Elizabeth decides to surprise George with a candlelight dinner. She gets home early, cooks a 3-course meal, and sets the table. After getting ready, she takes a seat at the table and waits for George to arrive. However, when he's half an hour late, she calls him to find out what's delaying him. However, he doesn't pick up the phone. A few hours later, George walks into the house exhausted. He sees the dinner spread and immediately feels guilty. The moment Elizabeth sees him, she starts shouting that he ruined date night. Even though George had no idea that Elizabeth had planned this surprise, he feels upset. On the other hand, Elizabeth starts to question whether staying in this relationship is worth it or not. Maybe, she is settling for less.*

One transgression does not speak for your relationship! In her anger, Elizabeth forgot all the good times she had spent with George. This doesn't mean that the relationship isn't going well.

Your expectations can be yours and your relationship's downfall. If you were to find yourself in such a situation, here's what you need to focus on:

- *Your partner makes you laugh*
- *Your partner does not shout at you or call you names when you are fighting*
- *Your partner is happy with your financial success*
- *Your partner has got your back and pushes you to achieve your dreams*

The word "enough" here does not translate to compromise. It means that you are happy with what you have. Again, this doesn't mean that you shouldn't strive for more but expecting everything from your partner is where you are wrong. If the tables were turned, how would you feel? Maybe, your partner does not feel satisfied with what you do and how you display your affection. Gives you something to think about, doesn't it?

So, what drives the train of a good-enough relationship?

It's simple — two bogies:  realistic and unrealistic expectations.

Realistic expectations are those that you deserve and unrealistic are those that make you feel content on the surface. Couples believe that without the toppings (unrealistic expectations); they won't have any happiness in their relationship.

Our advice – ~~don't~~ have ~~high~~ expectations!

People who expect certain things from their partners are always treated like a king/queen. Those who don't are treated poorly. So, do have expectations but just make sure they are real and not some fairytale version of a movie.

Hoping for respect, kindness, and love in a relationship are realistic expectations. However, hoping for big gestures or expensive gifts is unrealistic. The latter is usually attached to money, as well as attention.

## How to Have a Good-Enough Relationship

Let's talk about what you can do to change your mindset. Letting go of unrealistic expectations is difficult but not impossible. Reaching contentment is all about believing in your partner and coming to the realization that what you have is something many people crave for. So, consider yourself lucky.

Below are a couple of tips on how to have a good-enough relationship:

In simple words, a good-enough relationship is all about reaching contentment. To be happy with your partner, you need to look at the small things because they matter.

*Tip #1 – Your Relationship IS Perfect… Believe That*

Every couple experiences ups and downs in their life. You will fight with each other, then make up and laugh about it later. You have probably heard the saying, "No relationship is perfect" and that's true but what's the harm in believing in the opposite? When you assume that your relationship is perfect, you don't go to extreme lengths to make your partner happy and that's a good thing. Why?

Because one of you will always fall short and that will build resentment. A little perfection simply pushes you to strive for the best that makes you both happy.

*Tip #2 – Be Grateful for Such a Loving Partner*

You have someone who loves you, takes care of you, and is willing to do anything for you. Those late-night cuddles, anniversary and birthday gifts, and whatnot... be thankful that you have such a partner in your life.

*Tip #3 – Stop Focusing on the Little Things*

Some people have this bad habit of picking apart their relationship, not because they are not satisfied with their partner but because they have made up their mind that they no longer feel happy.

*"I hate when he always orders Chinese! Doesn't he know that I like Italian?"*

*"She keeps nagging me to pick up my socks. It's my house too! I can put them wherever I want."*

If your thinking follows a somewhat similar pattern then you need to stop those thoughts immediately. Answer this first — do you want to continue in your relationship?

If yes then let's keep moving forward.

When such a negative thought crosses your mind, replace it with something good about your partner.

*"So what if he likes Chinese more? Whenever we go out, he makes sure that we eat Italian."*

*"So what if she nags me. I am grateful that she does my laundry. I will try not to give her any grief over this next time."*

*Tip #4 – Enjoy the Little Things*

When it comes to the small things that bother you, you need to think happy thoughts about your partner to displace them. However, when it comes to the little things your partner does to make you happy, you need to pay more attention and show gratitude.

For example, it's your birthday and you were expecting a big surprise with an expensive gift and a romantic dinner in a 5-star restaurant. However, your partner invited your friends over to the house and ordered takeout. This gesture, though thoughtful on his end, was not something that you wanted. Notice how we mentioned "thoughtful?" And that's what matters! You don't need fancy words or gifts to feel loved. Love comes from the heart so look at the effort your partner put into the planning and be thankful for it.

## Step #5 – Enjoy the Present

Often couples jump into the future even before their present relationship is solidified? Stop thinking about buying a house or having babies when you have barely learned each other's likes and dislikes. Also, stop reliving the past! Yes, the courtship stage of your relationship was magical but now, you need to focus on more important things to find out how you can solidify your relationship.

The past has the power to bring out old hurts and the future will just make you anxious when you will fail to achieve a goal. So, start living in the present. "Now" is what matters the most so make the best of it!

In a way, you can say that having a good-enough relationship trumps being the perfect couple. Just because you don't finish each other's sentences doesn't mean that you don't have a strong bond. If you both love and respect each other and take care of each other's needs and wants then you have nothing to worry about.

## Display of Affection – Show Your Love, Feel Their Love

Romance has the power to make everything… alright.

Your partner is pouting? A bouquet of roses will go a long way in making them feel loved.

Your partner is angry? Cook them their favorite meal because the way to a person's heart is through their stomach… No kidding!

Love is a feeling that always has you in a romantic mood. If you are always figuring out ways to put a smile on your partner's face and sparkle in their eyes then you are on the right track to showing your love.

Remember — a big gesture does not always show love. If your partner feels the same way about you as you do about them then they will be happy with a single rose instead of a bouquet of 24. It's your thought that you put into the gesture that matters.

For some couples, the display of affection whether in private or public, never comes easily. That's because they are afraid of rejection. If you are looking for some guide sent down from heaven to help you with this dilemma then you won't find any. No need to go all-in because, in a scenario where your partner does not like what you do, you won't feel disappointed. Couples grow in a relationship and their personalities change over time. What your partner liked at the start of the relationship, they might not like now. So, start doing what comes naturally to you.

You do need to put in extra effort to show your love otherwise, your partner will feel that whatever you are doing is simply out of obligation. People fall in love in a matter of seconds. However, falling out takes time, which is why you can do a lot to get your relationship back on track. Before your relationship comes to this point, which does not work on closing the cracks?

Following are five ways on how to romance your partner:

### 1.   Have the Dessert at Home

Did you get the double entendre? It's often shown in movies that after having dinner, the tension between a couple builds up to a point where they can't wait for dessert. "Wink"

So, get that dessert to go and have a great time with it at home, and by that we mean, licking it off your… if you know what we mean.

### 2.   Memorize the Important Dates

Yes, we are talking about all those important dates such as when you first met, when you said "I Love You," birthdays, anniversaries, and whatnot. Do whatever you can to show your love during these days because a gesture at such an occasion will be more meaningful than your daily kisses and love declarations.

### 3.   Kiss Your Partner Senseless

Your partner is sitting on the couch, watching TV. Walk up to them and lay one down that will shut their capacity for thinking. Then, don't utter a word, and just walk away. Trust us, this will work like a charm, and you will be on their mind the entire day.

### 4.   Indulge in Public Display of Affective (PDA)

Holding hands while running errands, a light smooch on the lips, a kiss on the cheek, grazing their things with your fingertips… all these gestures will make your partner feel desired. Need we say more?

### 5.  Do a Striptease

Alright, ladies and gentlemen! It's time to whip out your grooving skills. You don't need to go all Magic Mike on your partner but a little one step back and two steps forward will do the trick. What will this do? Get your partner in the mood and put a smile on their face the entire day!

Love is simple. It's us who complicates it? Is it difficult to tell your partner that you love them and are thankful for having them in your life? Yes, the words are a bit daunting but once you say them out loud, displaying other affections will come naturally.

## Conclusion

Couples who are secure in their relationships have immense respect for each other. They do argue and fight with each other but they never hit below the belt. Their relationship isn't toxic because both maintain their integrity.

Learn how to give space to your partner so that they can be themselves. Never be codependent because that way, you won't grow in your relationship. Saying that being open with your affection is difficult but at least try to show your partner that you are there for them. Pick your battles wisely and don't let arguments turn into a shouting match.

The start of every new relationship is very exciting. The first touch, the first kiss, and that first intimate look that sweeps you off your feet — those are just the surface emotions. To make your relationship last longer, you need to dig deeper. Once you are committed to your relationship, time starts… to not take each other for granted.

This is why to bring back the spark in your relationship, you need to put in continuous effort. The signs we mentioned at the start of this guide will tell you that you are slowly falling out of love. You might have also noticed that we have placed immense importance on communication, which is the key that locks a relationship. Without it, your relationship is bound to fade into the nothingness of comfort.

So, show your love, shout it at the top of your lungs and be there for your partner every step of the way.

# Bibliography

Tamsen Firestone, (2014), _How Do I Know if I Have a Fantasy Bond?_ Psych Alive

Mackenzie Dunn, (2019), _8 Signs You Might Be Falling Out of Love_, Woman's Day

Stacey Laura Lloyd, (2020), _6 Signs You May Be Falling Out of Love With Your S.O. & What To Do About It_, Brides

Lybi Ma, (2021), _10 Subtle Signs You Are Falling Out of Love_, Psychology Today

Jonita Dsouza, (2017), _4 Stepping Stones for a Lasting Love Relationship_, Exploring Feminity